Nat

STO   S

Revised & Updated
By Nathan Levy

A collection of original thinking activities for improving inquiry!

An N.L. Associates, Inc. book

Copyright © 2005 N.L. Associates, Inc.

All rights reserved. No part of this book may be reproduced in any manner whatever, including information storage or retrieval, in whole or in part (except for brief quotations in critical articles or reviews), without written permission from the publisher. For more information, write to:

    N.L. Associates, Inc.
    PO Box 1199
    Hightstown, NJ 08520-0399

Library of Congress Catalog Number
89-92195
ISBN 1-878347-64-0

Copyright © 2005 N.L. Associates, Inc.

Printed in the United States of America

PREFACE – by Nathan Levy

This book is the result of several years' accumulation of ideas leading to puzzling stories that lend themselves to what I call thinking games. The "games" have become the means for thousands of people to carry on a totally enjoyable process of engaging critical and imaginative thinking. Volume 1 of my Stories with Holes is a collection of stories that has been gathered from various sources. Nathan Levy's Stories with Holes Volumes 2-20 are original. Wherever I speak I share some of the stories with my training groups. Teachers, parents and children enjoy the stories immensely. I hope you will as well.

INTRODUCTION

The objectives of using Nathan Levy's Stories with Holes include the following:

- to provide for growth in imagination and intuitive functioning
- to give experiences that display the fun of working cooperatively, rather than competitively, on a common problem
- to increase cognitive skills of resolving discrepancies through successful experiences
- to provide enjoyable changes-of-pace for task-oriented learning environments

This is a structured activity. It is designed to ensure involvement on the part of each participant, and to promote feelings of group and individual success.

The games are designed to accommodate all levels. "Children" from ages 8-88 will benefit from using these stories.

The time a story takes will vary. Usually a story lasts from 3 to 30 minutes, but some stories can take days. Children, lower grades through high school, tend to regard these thinking games as play instead of work. It is one of the few activities I know of that "hooks" almost anyone into creative use of their intelligence, i.e. learning, almost in spite of themselves. <u>Nathan Levy's Stories with Holes</u> are for all groups over age seven, regardless of background or achievement level.

**Please note that I have revised the above introduction and the following methodology from the way they appeared in the original collection of <u>Stories with Holes.</u> The revisions are based on my current workshop experiences with children and adults.

N.L.

METHODOLOGY

The first time a group plays, it will be necessary to begin by announcing something like the following: "I am going to tell you a story with a hole in it – I mean that an important part of the story is missing. Listen carefully so you can find the missing part, for the story may not seem to make much sense to you at first..."

At this point, tell the story once, pause, and then tell it the same way again. Then say...

"You can ask questions that can be answered either with a "yes" or with a "no". I can only answer "yes", "no", "does not compute", or "is not relevant". If I answer, "does not compute", that means that the question you asked cannot receive a straight "yes" or "no" without throwing you off the track."

Allow for questions about the process, if there are any, but usually it is best simply to jump into the game by having the questioning start. The process becomes clear as the game progresses. Once a group has played the game, the full directions given above for playing the game are unnecessary.

From this point on, answer only in one of the four designated ways. The following is an example of a computed story taken from <u>Stories with Holes</u>, and how it might be played:

Story: Mitch lives on the twentieth floor of an apartment building. Every time he leaves, he rides a self-service elevator from the twentieth floor to the street; but every time he returns, he rides the same self-service elevator only to the fifteenth floor, where he leaves the elevator and walks up the remaining five flights of stairs. Repeat, then ask who knows the answer already; if any do, ask them to observe and not give away the answer.

Question: Does the elevator go all the way up?
Answer: Yes.
Q: Does he want the exercise?
A: No.
Q: Does it have something to do with the elevator not working right?
A: No.
Q: Does he have a girlfriend on the 15th floor who he stops to see?
A: No.
Q: Does he have something different about him?
A: Yes.
Q: Is he a robber?
A: No.
Q: Is he a real person?
A: Yes.
Q: A tall person?
A: No.
Q: Is his size important?
A: Yes.
Q: I know! He's too short to reach the button!
A: Right!

v

At this point, make certain that all the participants understand the answer and why it is the correct answer. In the example given above, the group found the answer quite soon. Instead of starting a new game -- particularly if this is the first time playing – spend some time processing the game with questions like:

* What did you have to do in order to play this game? (Listen, hear each answer, think, imagine, follow a line of reasoning, eliminate possibilities, etc.)

* Ask the person who finally solved the riddle, "Joanne, did you have help from others in finding the answer?" It nearly always comes out that the person relied on previous questions and answers. Use this to point out the interdependence of players, and reduce competition within the group to be the "winner".

* When do you see yourself having to use the kind of thinking you use in this game?

Usually a group of youngsters will be eager to try a second game right away.

Some important points to remember:

1. Immediately following the telling of each story and before the questioning begins, ask if anyone in the group has heard it before and knows the answer. Tell these people to observe and refrain from questioning.

2. Use the "does not compute" response whenever a single word or phrase in a question makes it impossible to answer with a "yes" or "no" answer. Examples from the story above:

- "Why does he live on the twentieth floor?" "Why" questions, as well as "where, who, when or which", cannot be answered "yes" or "no".

- "Does the elevator operator make him get off at the fifteenth floor?" No mention was made of an operator.

3. If a game goes past 10 or 12 minutes and some people begin to lose interest close the game for the present. There is absolutely nothing harmful in leaving the puzzle unsolved. The group can return to it another time, when interest and energy are high. Some students may protest, but do not give the answer. The experience of non-closure provides some valuable learning in itself; but more importantly, once a group has expended considerable energy on the game, the victory should be an earned one. Although there may be some unusual circumstances under which you would give the group the answer, I have found it best not to do so (even if some are begging). The point here is not to "take the answer away by giving it." You can always return to it later. What is important is that the students earn the feeling of "we-did-it!"

4. Share the computer (leader) role. Once kids have learned how the game works, have a volunteer lead the game. He or she must choose from the stories he

or she already knows. As soon as you are convinced the student is familiar with the story, the answer, and the process (which you should previously have modeled) have the leader read the story to the class and begin taking questions. Most important here is what you model. A child-led computer game is an excellent small-group activity to have going on while you are occupied elsewhere in the classroom.

5. You may periodically want to encourage categorical thinking. When a player asks a question beginning, "Would it help us to know…" or "Does it have anything to do with…" pause in the game and show how the type of question is uniquely helpful in narrowing down the range of questions, distilling and focusing the group's attention, or cutting away large slices of the topic that are irrelevant. Thus, the question "Is David's occupation important?" tends to be more useful than "Is he a plumber? A teacher?", etc.

6. Be sure that a question is exactly true, or exactly false, before responding. One word can make the difference.

1. Cindy's Glass

Cindy forgot to look at the timekeeper and dropped her glass when the ball was thrown.

Answer:

Cinderella lost her glass slipper at midnight.

2. King Ammon

When King Ammon died, all the members of the Royal Family refused to attend the funeral services.

Answer:

The Royal Family (Paul, Mary Ann, Danielle, Alex and Dennis Royal) did not like King Ammon and refused to go to the funeral.

3. Ms. Pazinko's Sitting

Ms. Pazinko was sitting in the school lounge with a cup of tea. Looking out the window, she saw Alfie F. and Johnny C. taking swings at each other. Ms. Pazinko quickly picked up her cup and went to take a closer look at the two boys, but did not separate them.

Answer:

Alfie and Johnny were playing tennis.

4. Charles the Cat

Charles The Cat swallowed the bug and died.

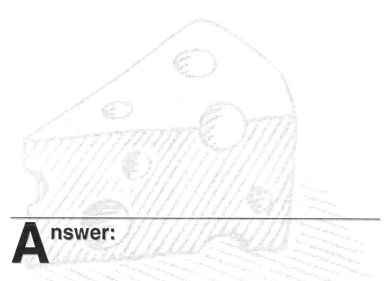

Answer:

Charles the Cat was a catfish who swallowed a "fly" from a fishing rod.

5. Joanie, the Old Horse

Joanie, the Old Horse with brown colored spots, was bucking up and down then stopped without a neigh or whinny!

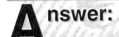

Answer:

Joanie, the Old Horse, was a Mustang car that stopped working.

6. Maria, Debbie and Maryann on the Island

After almost two hours, Maria, Debbie and Maryann were on the edge of a tiny island waiting for help. They saw a boat coming their way. The boat approached the island. The man at the controls saw the three teenagers, but did not help them.

Answer:

Maria, Debbie and Maryann were hitchhiking. The island was a grassy area in the middle of a road. The driver of the car was pulling a large boat behind him as he drove past the hitchhikers.

7. Young Mark

Young Mark started to cry as the boat approached.

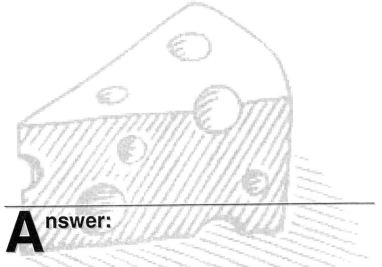

Answer:

Young Mark, a boy of six, was afraid of doctors. He had heard his mother say that the boat was approaching the dock.

8. The Attack

The soldiers attacked even though the female opponents were unarmed. The captain savagely stabbed several. Neither the captain, nor the soldiers were punished for their insensitive acts.

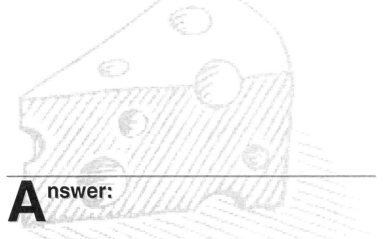

Answer:

A group of soldiers were eating chicken breasts for dinner.

9. A World Comes Apart

The world came apart. Asia was in the worst shape of all. Devin was the hero who helped fix the world.

Answer:

Devin D'Arcangelo was the man who put the puzzle of the world back together after the dog messed it up.

9

10. A Tear in the Knee

When the creative comedian acted as if his humorous jokes were being told by a knee tear in his pants, Barbara Oxenhorn remembered the name of a great inventor.

Answer:

Barbara remembered Eli Whitney (Wit-Knee), the inventor of the cotton gin.

11. Dominique Running

Dominique was running quickly when she fell down and continued running, even faster. Then she disappeared. What was the fate of Dominique?

Answer:

Dominique is a river that flowed into the ocean.

11

12. Elaine's Body Parts

When Glen arrived, Elaine's body parts were scattered everywhere, although no blood had been shed.

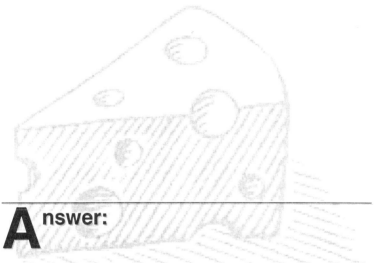

Answer:

Elaine was Glen's Cadillac, being put back together in a garage after a serious accident.

13. The Magnificent Queen

The magnificent Queen was brought to the hotel wearing a beautiful dress. When she arrived in her room, she did not leave for two years.

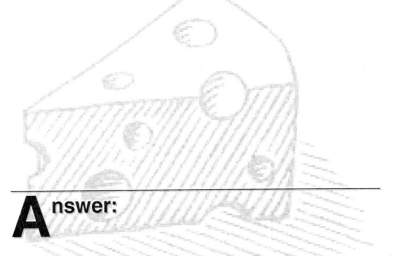

Answer:

The magnificent Queen was a queen sized bed with a beautiful spread. The bed was delivered to the new hotel and stayed in the room for two years.

14. Stacy and Lisa

Stacy and Lisa went to several clubs but did no dancing.

Answer:

Stacy and Lisa were golfers.

14

15. Joey's Snapped Suspenders

Joey's snapped suspenders caused a problem. His pants were not fine—and neither was Joey.

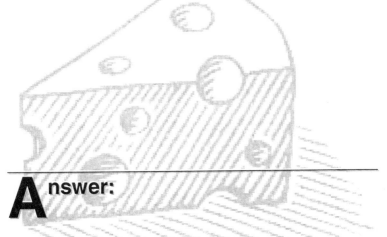

Answer:

Joey is a bungee jumper. His "suspender" snapped and he jumped into the bay for an unexpected swim.

16. The Accident

There was nothing Leonard the driver could do about the impending crash of the car he was driving. Leonard knew he was in danger. Even though the car was completely demolished, there was not a scratch on him.

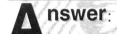

Answer:

Leonard had used his brother's new remote control car without asking. Leonard was saved when his parents protected him from his older brother who had discovered the damage to his new car.

17. Joanie – the Famous Mountain Climber

While alone on a mountain, Joanie Kreid, the famous mountain climber dropped 300 feet. She was not wearing any protective garments and she was not using any ropes. Yet Joanie was not killed or injured.

Answer:

The 300 feet Joanie dropped were lucky rabbit's feet she had been carrying in a bag on her way to a store on top of the mountain. The store sold rabbit's feet.

18. Ike and Edna

Ike's carelessness with the sharp object caused Sue to lose her eye while at Edna's house. Edna was relaxed about the event even though her family was horrified.

Answer:

Sue was a potato. The family thought that Edna's entry for most perfect potato in the State Fair was damaged by Ike. Edna was calm because the potato she was entering, Marci Potato, was safely packed in another place.

19. Thieves

The masked thieves grabbed the money from the defenseless woman. The woman immediately wished the thieves good luck.

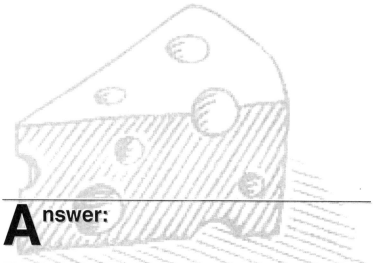

Answer:

The masked thieves were young trick-or-treaters during Halloween.

19

20. Dr. Stoller's Meal

Dr. Stoller, a medical doctor, was sitting at the restaurant table with his friends. Shortly after the completion of the meal, Dr. Stoller was no longer a doctor.

Answer:

The contents of the meal made Dr. Stoller very sick. He was rushed to the hospital where he became a patient.

ABOUT THE AUTHOR

Nathan Levy

Nathan Levy is the author of more than 40 books which have sold almost 250,000 copies to teachers and parents in the US, Europe, Asia, South America, Australia and Africa. His unique <u>Stories with Holes</u> series continues to be proclaimed the most popular activity used in gifted, special education and regular classrooms by hundreds of educators. An extremely popular, dynamic speaker on thinking, writing and differentiation, Nathan is in high demand as a workshop leader in school and business settings. As a former school principal, company president, parent of four daughters and management trainer, Nathan's ability to transfer knowledge and strategies to audiences through humorous, thought provoking stories assures that participants leave with a plethora of new ways to approach their future endeavors.

NL Associates is pleased to be the publisher of this book. Teachers, students and other readers are invited to contribute their own "Stories with Holes" for possible inclusion in future volumes. Suggested stories will not be returned to you and will be acknowledged only if selected. Please send your suggestions to:

NL Associates Inc
PO Box 1199
Hightstown NJ 08520-0399
www.storieswithholes.com

Dynamic Speakers
Creative Workshops
Relevant Topics

Nathan Levy, author of the Stories with Holes series and There Are Those, and other nationally known authors and speakers, can help your school or organization achieve positive results with children. We can work with you to provide a complete in-service package or have one of our presenters lead one of several informative and entertaining workshops.

Workshop Topics Include:

- Practical Activities for Teaching Gifted Children
- Differentiating in the Regular Classroom
- How to Help Children Read, Write and Think Better
- Using Stories with Holes and Other Thinking Activities
- Powerful Strategies to Enhance Learning
- Communicating Better in the Workplace
- Communicating Better at Home
- Communicating Better at School
- The Principal as an Educational Leader
    and many more…

Other Titles By Nathan Levy

Not Just Schoolwork
Volumes 1-4

Write, From the
Beginning
(*Revised Edition*)

Thinking and Writing
Activities for the Brain!
Books 1 and 2

Creativity Day-by-Day
(Stimulating Activities
for Kids and Adults)

Stories with Holes
Volumes 1-20

Intriguing Questions
Volumes 1-6

Whose Clues
Volumes 1-6

Nathan Levy's
Test Booklet of Basic
Knowledge for Every
American Over 9 Years
Old

There Are Those

101 Things Everyone
Should Know About
Science

Stories with Holes
Gift Set
Volumes 1-12
Sample stories taken from 19 of the 20 original volumes of Stories with Holes. Some of the more difficult stories have been omitted. The glossy covers make this set more appropriate as a gift.

Please write or call to receive our current catalog.
**NL Associates, Inc.
P.O. Box 1199
Hightstown, NJ 08520-0399
(732) 656 - 7822
www.storieswithholes.com**